KT-226-156

Shakespeare
THE ANIMATED TALES

AS YOU LIKE IT

ABRIDGED BY LEON GARFIELD

ILLUSTRATED BY VALENTIN OLSCHWANG

HEINEMANN YOUNG BOOKS

William Shakespeare

Martin Droeshout sculpsit London.

WILLIAM SHAKESPEARE

NEXT TO GOD, A wise man once said, Shakespeare created most. In the thirty-seven plays that are his chief legacy to the world – and surely no-one ever left a richer! – human nature is displayed in all its astonishing variety.

He has enriched the stage with matchless comedies, tragedies, histories, and, towards the end of his life, with plays that defy all description, strange plays that haunt the imagination like visions.

His range is enormous: kings and queens, priests, princes and merchants, soldiers, clowns and drunkards, murderers, pimps, whores, fairies, monsters and pale, avenging ghosts 'strut and fret their hour upon the stage'. Murders and suicides abound; swords flash, blood flows, poison drips, and lovers sigh; yet there is always time for old men to talk of growing apples and for gardeners to discuss the weather.

In the four hundred years since they were written, they have become known and loved in every land; they are no longer the property of one country and one people, they are the priceless possession of the world.

His life, from what we know of it, was not astonishing. The stories that have attached themselves to him are remarkable only for their ordinariness: poaching deer, sleeping off a drinking bout under a wayside tree. There are no duels, no loud, passionate loves, no excesses of any kind. He was not one of your unruly geniuses whose habits are more interesting than their works. From all accounts, he was of a gentle, honourable disposition, a good businessman, and a careful father.

He was born on April 23rd 1564, to John and Mary Shakespeare of Henley Street, Stratford-upon-Avon. He was their third child and first son. When he was four or five he began his education at the local petty school. He left the local grammar school when he was about fourteen, in all probability to help in his father's glove-making shop. When he was eighteen, he married Anne Hathaway, who lived in a nearby village. By the time he was twenty-one, he was the father of three children, two daughters and a son.

Then, it seems, a restless mood came upon him. Maybe he travelled, maybe he was, as some say, a schoolmaster in the country; but at some time during the next seven years, he went to London and found employment in the theatre. When he was twenty-eight, he was already well enough known as an actor and playwright to excite the spiteful envy of a rival, who referred to him as 'an upstart crow'.

He mostly lived and worked in London until his mid-forties, when he returned to his family and home in Stratford, where he remained in prosperous circumstances until his death on April 23rd 1616, his fifty-second birthday.

He left behind him a widow, two daughters (his son died in childhood), and the richest imaginary world ever created by the human mind.

LEON GARFIELD

The list of the plays contained in the First Folio of 1623. This was the first collected edition of Shakespeare's plays and was gathered together by two of his fellow actors, John Hemmings and Henry Condell.

A CATALOGVE

of the severall Comedies, Histories, and Tragedies contained in this Volume.

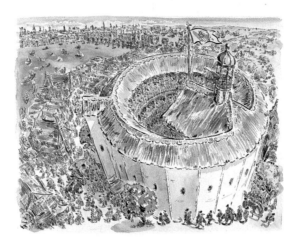

The Theatre in Shakespeare's Day

IN 1989 AN ARCHAEOLOGICAL discovery was made on the south bank of the Thames that sent shivers of delight through the theatre world. A fragment of Shakespeare's own theatre, the Globe, where many of his plays were first performed, had been found.

This discovery has fuelled further interest in how Shakespeare himself conceived and staged his plays. We know a good deal already, and archaeology as well as documentary research will no doubt reveal more, but although we can only speculate on some of the details, we have a good idea of what the Elizabethan theatre-goer saw, heard and smelt when he went to see a play by William Shakespeare at the Globe.

It was an entirely different experience from anything we know today. Modern theatres have roofs to keep out the weather. If it rained on the Globe, forty per cent of the play-goers got wet. Audiences today sit on cushioned seats, and usually (especially if the play is by Shakespeare) watch and listen in respectful silence. In the Globe, the floor of the theatre was packed with a riotous crowd of garlic-reeking apprentices, house servants and artisans, who had each paid a penny to stand for the entire duration of the play, to buy nuts and apples from the food-sellers, to refresh themselves with bottled ale, relieve themselves, perhaps, into buckets by the back wall, to talk, cheer, catcall, clap and hiss if the play did not please them.

The Globe Theatre

In the galleries that rose in curved tiers around the inside of the building sat those who could afford to pay two pennies for a seat, and the benefits of a roof over their heads. Here, the middle ranking citizens, the merchants, the sea captains, the clerks from the Inns of Court, would sit crammed into their small eighteen inch space and look down upon the 'groundlings' below. In the 'Lords' room', the rich and the great, noblemen and women, courtiers and foreign ambassadors had to pay sixpence each for the relative comfort and luxury of their exclusive position directly above the stage, where they smoked tobacco, and overlooked the rest.

We are used to a stage behind an arch, with wings on either side, from which the actors come on and into which they disappear. In the Globe, the stage was a platform thrusting out into the middle of the floor, and the audience, standing in the central yard, surrounded it on three sides. There were no wings. Three doors at the back of the stage were used for all exits and entrances. These were sometimes covered by a curtain, which could be used as a prop.

The Workes of William Shakespeare,

containing all his Comedies, Histories, and
Tragedies: Truely set forth, according to their first
ORIGINALL.

The Names of the Principall Actors
in all these Playes.

Illiam Shakespeare.

Richard Burbadge.

John Hemmings.

Augustine Phillips.

William Kempt.

Thomas Poope.

George Bryan.

Henry Condell.

William Slye.

Richard Cowly.

John Lowine.

Samuell Crosse.

Alexander Cooke.

Samuel Gilburne.

Robert Armin.

William Ostler.

Nathan Field.

John Underwood.

Nicholas Tooley.

William Ecclestone.

Joseph Taylor.

Robert Benfield.

Robert Goughe.

Richard Robinson.

Iohn Shancke.

Iohn Rice.

From this list of actors, we can see that William Shakespeare not only wrote plays but also acted in them. The Globe theatre, where these actors performed, is now being rebuilt close to its original site on the south bank of the river Thames.

Today we sit in a darkened theatre or cinema, and look at a brilliantly lit stage or screen, or we sit at home in a small, private world of our own, watching a luminous television screen. The close-packed, rowdy crowd at the Globe, where the play started at two o'clock in the afternoon, had no artificial light to enhance their illusion. It was the words that moved them. They came to listen, rather than to see.

No dimming lights announced the start of the play. A blast from a trumpet and three sharp knocks warned the audience that the action was about to begin. In the broad daylight, the actor could see the audience as clearly as the audience could see him. He spoke directly to the crowd, and held them with his eyes, following their reactions. He could play up to the raucous laughter that greeted the comical, bawdy scenes, and gauge the emotional response to the higher flights of poetry. Sometimes he even improvised speeches of his own. He was surrounded by, enfolded by, his audience.

The stage itself would seem uncompromisingly bare to our eyes. There was no scenery. No painted backdrops suggested a forest, or a castle, or the sumptuous interior of a palace. Shakespeare painted the scenery with his words, and the imagination of the audience did the rest.

Props were brought onto the stage only when they were essential for the action. A bed would be carried on when a character needed to lie on it. A throne would be let down from above when a king needed to sit on it. Torches and lanterns would suggest that it was dark, but the main burden of persuading an audience, at three o'clock in the afternoon, that it was in fact the middle of the night, fell upon the language.

In our day, costume designers create a concept as part of the production of a play into which each costume fits. Shakespeare's actors were responsible for their own costumes. They would use what was to hand in the 'tiring house' (dressing room), or supplement it out of their own pockets. Classical, medieval and Tudor clothes could easily appear side by side in the same play.

No women actors appeared on a public stage until many years after Shakespeare's death, for at that time it would have been considered shameless. The parts of young girls were played by boys. The parts of older women were played by older men.

In 1613 the Globe theatre was set on fire by a spark from a cannon during a performance of Henry VIII, and it burnt to the ground. The actors, including Shakespeare himself, dug into their own pockets and paid for it to be rebuilt. The new theatre lasted until 1642, when it closed again. Now, in the 1990s, the Globe is set to rise again as a committed band of actors, scholars and enthusiasts are raising the money to rebuild Shakespeare's theatre in its original form a few yards from its previous site.

From the time when the first Globe theatre was built until today, Shakespeare's plays have been performed in a vast variety of languages, styles, costumes and techniques, on stage, on film, on television and in animated film. Shakespeare himself, working within the round wooden walls of his theatre, would have been astonished by it all.

PATRICK SPOTTISWOODE
Director of Education,
Globe Theatre Museum

SHAKESPEARE TODAY

SHAKESPEARE IS ALIVE TODAY! Although William Shakespeare the man lies long buried in Stratford-upon-Avon parish church, he lives on in countless millions of hearts and minds.

Imagine that cold April day in 1616. The small funeral procession labours slowly along Church Street. Huge black horses draw the wooden cart bearing the simple coffin. On the coffin, a few daffodils and primroses, plucked only minutes before from the garden of New Place, gravely nod with each jolt and jar of the rutted road.

Most of Stratford's citizens have turned out, muffled against the biting wind, to see the last appearance of their wealthy neighbour. You couldn't call it a crowd. Just small respectful groups clustering the dry places on the roadside, careful to avoid the mud splashed up by the great hooves of the lumbering horses.

Men and women briefly bow their heads as the dead man and the black-clad mourners pass. The townspeople share their opinions, as neighbours do. "He used to do some acting, didn't he?" "Made a lot of money in London. Writing plays, I think." "Used to come home once a year to see his family, but nobody here really knew a lot about Master Shakespeare." "Wasn't he a poet?" "Big landowner hereabouts anyway. All those fields over at Welcombe."

Past the Guild Chapel where he had worshipped as a boy. Past the school where long ago his imagination was fired by language. At the churchyard gate, under the sad elms, six men effortlessly heave the coffin on to their shoulders. William Shakespeare is about to enter his parish church for the last time.

Nobody at that long ago funeral guessed that they were saying goodbye to a man who would become the most famous Englishman of his age – perhaps of all time.

Shakespeare lives on. He weaves familiar themes into his tales: the conflicts between parents and children, love at first sight, the power struggles of war and politics. His language is heard everywhere. If you ever call someone 'a blinking idiot' or 'a tower of strength', or describe them as 'tongue-tied', or suffering from 'green-eyed jealousy', or being 'dead as a doornail', you are speaking the language of Shakespeare.

If you say 'it was Greek to me' or 'parting is such sweet sorrow', or that something is 'too much of a good thing' and that you 'have not slept one wink', the words of Shakespeare are alive in your mouth. Shakespeare's language has a power all of its own, rich in emotional intensity. Because he was a poet who wrote plays, he could make even the simplest words utterly memorable. All around the world people know Hamlet's line 'To be or not to be, that is the question.'

Shakespeare is still performed today because of the electrifying power of his storytelling. Whether his story is about love or murder, or kings and queens, he keeps you on the edge of your seat wanting to know what happens next.

He created well over nine hundred characters in his plays. However large or small the part, each character springs vividly to life in performance. They live in our imagination because they are so much like people today. They experience the same emotions that everyone feels and recognises: love, jealousy, fear, courage, ambition, pride ... and a hundred others.

In every play, Shakespeare invites us to imagine what the characters are like, and for nearly four hundred years people have accepted Shakespeare's invitation. The plays have been re-imagined in very many ways. They have been shortened, added to, and set in very different periods of history. They have been translated into many languages and performed all over the world. Shakespeare lives because all persons in every age and every society can make their own interpretations and performances of Shakespeare.

The creators of *The Animated Tales* have re-imagined *As You Like It* in a 26 minute animated film. You too can make your own living Shakespeare. Read the text that follows, and watch the video. Then try reading the play either by yourself, changing your voice to suit the different characters, or with friends, and record it on a tape recorder. If you have a toy theatre, try staging it with characters and scenery that you make and paint yourself. Or collect together a cast and create your own production for your family and friends.

DR REX GIBSON

Dr Rex Gibson is the director of the Shakespeare and Schools Project which is part of the Institute of Education at the University of Cambridge.

In 1994 he was awarded the Sam Wanamaker International Shakespeare Award for his outstanding contribution to the world's knowledge of the works of Shakespeare.

What They Said of Him

One will ever find, in searching his works, new cause for astonishment and admiration.

GOETHE

Shakespeare was a writer of all others the most calculated to make his readers better as well as wiser.

SAMUEL TAYLOR COLERIDGE

An overstrained enthusiasm is more pardonable with respect to Shakespeare than the want of it; for our admiration cannot easily surpass his genius.

WILLIAM HAZLITT

It required three hundred years for England to begin to hear those two words that the whole world cries in her ear – William Shakespeare.

VICTOR HUGO

He has left nothing to be said about nothing or anything.

JOHN KEATS

The stream of time, which is continually washing the dissoluble fabrics of other poets, passes without injury by the adamant of Shakespeare.

SAMUEL JOHNSON

AS YOU LIKE IT

As You Like It tells a story that begins in the discord and violence of a tyrant's court, where broken ribs and brotherly hatred are the orders of the day, and moves to the strange, enchanted Forest of Arden, where all wounds are healed and all ills made good, where the very trees sprout love-poems ... It is a forest fairly infested with wandering lovers and outlaws who 'live like the old Robin Hood of England ... and fleet the time carelessly, as they did in the golden world.'

It is indeed a golden play, and at the very heart of it is Rosalind, a banished princess, who, with her companions in exile, seeks the young Orlando, who, as her cousin puts it, "tripped up the wrestler's heels, and your heart, both in an instant!"

THE CHARACTERS IN THE PLAY

in order of appearance

DUKE FREDERICK	*usurper of Duke Senior*
ROSALIND	*daughter to Duke Senior*
CHARLES	*Duke Frederick's wrestler*
ORLANDO	*son of Sir Rowland de Boys*
CELIA	*daughter to Duke Frederick*
OLIVER	*son of Sir Rowland de Boys*
DUKE SENIOR	*living in exile*
LORD	*attending on Duke Senior*
ADAM	*an old servant of Sir Rowland de Boys*
TOUCHSTONE	*a Fool at Duke Frederick's court*
CORIN	*an old shepherd*
SILVIUS	*a shepherd*
AMIENS	*a lord attending Duke Senior*
JAQUES	*a lord attending Duke Senior*
AUDREY	*a goat-herd*
PHEBE	*a shepherdess*
HYMEN	*the god of marriage*
MESSENGER	

Lords, servants and other attendants, shepherds and shepherdesses

The curtain rises on a lawn before the palace. There is to be a wrestling match before Duke Frederick and all his court. Already Charles, the strongest man in the country, has broken the ribs of three young men; now a fourth is awaited. Celia, the daughter of the duke, and Rosalind her cousin enter. They are followed by the duke and his courtiers, together with Charles the wrestler and Orlando, the fourth young man.

DUKE	How now, daughter and Rosalind? Are you crept hither to see the wrestling?
ROSALIND	Ay, uncle, so please you give us leave.
DUKE	You will take little delight in it, I can tell you, there is such odds in the man. In pity of the challenger's youth I would fain dissuade him, but he will not be entreated.

Duke Frederick gives a sign and Charles and Orlando begin to wrestle. The girls exclaim while watching.

ROSALIND	Now Hercules be thy speed, young man!
CELIA	I would I were invisible, to catch the strong fellow by the leg!

Charles is thrown.

ROSALIND	O excellent young man!

Shouts of amazement and admiration. Only one man hides himself angrily in the crowd – Oliver, Orlando's brother, who hates him.

DUKE	(*to Orlando*) What is thy name, young man?

ORLANDO   Orlando, my liege, the youngest son of Sir Rowland de Boys.

DUKE   I would thou hadst been son to some man else; the world
           esteem'd thy father honourable, but I did find him still mine
           enemy.

           *The duke departs barely suppressing his anger, followed by his
           court. Rosalind and Celia remain with Orlando.*

CELIA   My father's rough and envious disposition sticks me at the
           heart. (*They approach Orlando.*)

ROSALIND   (*giving him a chain from her neck*) Gentleman, wear this for
           me; one out of suits with Fortune, that could give more, but
           that her hand lacks means.

*Orlando is tongue-tied. Plainly, he and Rosalind have fallen in
love. Celia leads Rosalind away. Orlando gazes after them,
enraptured.*

Rosalind and Celia are together in their apartment.

CELIA   Come, come, wrestle with thy affections.

The duke enters furiously.

DUKE	Mistress, dispatch you with your safest haste, and get you from our court!
ROSALIND	Me, uncle?
DUKE	You, cousin. Within these ten days if that thou be'st found so near our public court as twenty miles, thou diest for it!
ROSALIND	I do beseech your Grace, let me the knowledge of my fault bear with me.
DUKE	Thou art thy father's daughter, there's enough.

He storms out.

CELIA	O my poor Rosalind, whither wilt thou go? Wilt thou change fathers? I will give thee mine. Say what thou canst, I'll go along with thee.
ROSALIND	Why, whither shall we go?
CELIA	To seek my uncle in the forest of Arden.
ROSALIND	Alas, what danger will it be to us? (*An idea seems to have struck Rosalind . . .*) But what if we assay'd . . .

Eagerly, they dress themselves for their adventure; Celia as a country maiden and Rosalind as a youth. They persuade Touchstone, the duke's jester, to bear them company in the forest.

CELIA   What shall I call thee when thou art a man?

ROSALIND   (*coming back in and putting on a hat*) Call me Ganymede. But what will you be called?

CELIA   (*coming in and putting on an apron*) No longer Celia, but Aliena.

In the forest of Arden Rosalind's father, once duke, but driven out by his younger brother Frederick, lives in banishment with a few faithful friends.

DUKE SENIOR   Now my brothers in exile, hath not old custom made this life more sweet than that of painted pomp? Are not these woods more free from peril than the envious court? And this our life finds tongues in trees, books in the running brooks, and good in everything. Where is Jaques?

LORD   We today did steal behind him as he lay under an oak, to which place a poor stag, that from the hunter's aim had ta'en a hurt, did come to languish. He swears that we are mere usurpers, tyrants, and what's worse, fright the animals and kill them in their native dwelling-place.

DUKE SENIOR   Show me the place. I love to hear him in these sullen fits.

The duke and lords ride off.

Orlando returns to his home and finds Adam, his old servant, waiting for him at the door.

ADAM   O unhappy youth, come not within these doors! Your brother hath heard your praises, and this night he means to burn the lodging where you use to lie, and you within it.

ORLANDO   Why, whither, Adam, wouldst thou have me go? Wouldst thou have me go and beg my food? Or with a base and boist'rous sword enforce a thievish living on the common road?

ADAM   But do not so! I have five hundred crowns I saved under your father. Take that.

ORLANDO   O good old man.

ADAM   Let me go with you. Though I look old, yet I am strong and lusty.

ORLANDO   Come, we'll go along together.

The three travellers, Rosalind, Celia and Touchstone, limp miserably through the forest. Rosalind, being dressed as a man, feels it her duty to present a bold and cheerful appearance.

ROSALIND   Well, this is the forest of Arden.

TOUCHSTONE   Ay, now am I in Arden, the more fool I. When I was at home, I was in a better place.

ROSALIND   Look you, who comes here.

They withdraw into concealment as Corin, an old shepherd and Silvius enter.

SILVIUS   O Corin, that thou knew'st how I do love her!

CORIN   I partly guess; for I have loved ere now.

SILVIUS   No, Corin, being old, thou canst not guess. O Phebe, Phebe, Phebe!

Silvius wanders away, distracted.

ROSALIND   Jove, Jove! This shepherd's passion is much upon my fashion! *(Rosalind leaves the shelter of the trees and approaches Corin.)* Good even to you, friend.

CORIN   And to you, gentle sir, and to you all.

ROSALIND   I prithee, shepherd, bring us where we may rest ourselves and feed. Here's a young maid with travel much oppress'd, and faints for succour.

CORIN   Fair sir, I pity her; but I am shepherd to another man. His cottage, flocks, and bounds of feed are now on sale, and there is nothing that you will feed on —

ROSALIND   I pray thee, if it stands with honesty, buy thou the cottage, pasture, and the flock, and thou shalt have to pay for it of us.

CELIA   And we will mend thy wages.

CORIN   I will your very faithful feeder be.

Another part of the forest. Orlando appears, assisting his old servant.

ADAM   Dear master, I can go no further. O, I die for food. Here lie I down and measure out my grave. Farewell, kind master.

ORLANDO   Why, how now, Adam? No greater heart in thee? Live a little, comfort a little, cheer thyself a little. If this uncouth forest yield anything savage, I will be either food for it, or bring it for food to thee.

Orlando unsheaths his sword and goes further into the forest. Hearing rustling in the grass, he stops and hides behind the bushes. A hound runs out and then runs deeper into the forest. Orlando follows the dog. He hears a song in the distance.

AMIENS
             Under the greenwood tree
             Who loves to lie with me,
             And turn his merry note
             Unto the sweet bird's throat,
             Come hither, come hither, come hither!
             Here shall he see
             No enemy
             But winter and rough weather.

He follows the 'Come hither', towards a glimmering of light and creeps to look between the foliage. The scene before him is of a banquet, lantern lit, and surrounded by gentlemen in comfortable furs. Among them is the melancholy Jaques. A hound lies at the feet of Duke Senior. The duke is about to sip from a goblet when he is interrupted.

ORLANDO (*rushing forward with drawn sword*) Forbear, and eat no more!

JAQUES Why, I have eat none yet.

ORLANDO Nor shalt not, till necessity be served.

DUKE SENIOR Sit down and feed, and welcome to our table.

ORLANDO (*putting up his sword*) Speak you so gently? Pardon me, I pray you. I thought that all things had been savage here. There is an old poor man —

DUKE SENIOR Go find him out, and we will nothing waste till your return.

ORLANDO (*departing*) I thank ye.

DUKE SENIOR   Thou seest we are not all alone unhappy: this wide and universal theatre presents more woeful pageants than the scene wherein we play.

JAQUES   All the world's a stage and all the men and women merely players. They have their exits and their entrances, and one man in his time plays many parts, his acts being seven ages. At first the infant . . . then the whining schoolboy . . . and then the lover. Then a soldier, jealous in honour, sudden, and quick in quarrel, and then the justice. The sixth age shifts into the lean and slipper'd pantaloon, with spectacles on nose. Last scene of all that ends this history, is second childishness, sans teeth, sans eyes, sans taste, sans everything.

As Jaques finishes his monologue, Orlando returns with Adam who is warmly welcomed, as if in contradiction of Jaques' grim view of old age.

At the palace, Duke Frederick discovers his daughter's flight with Rosalind; and, having heard of their talk with Orlando, suspects that they have all fled together. In a rage, he sends for Oliver, and orders him to find his brother Orlando or risk banishment himself.

In the forest Orlando has decorated all the trees he can find with poems of love to Rosalind.

ORLANDO   Hang there my verse, in witness of my love.

And away he goes in search of still more trees. No sooner has he gone than Rosalind appears with a poem in her hand.

ROSALIND   'From the east to western Inde,
No jewel is like Rosalind.
All the pictures fairest lin'd
Are but black to Rosalind.
Let no face be kept in mind
But the fair of Rosalind'.

Enter Celia, with another poem.

CELIA 'Thus Rosalind of many parts,
By heavenly synod was devis'd,
Of many faces, eyes, and hearts . . .'

TOUCHSTONE (*peeping out from behind a tree*) This is the very false gallop of verses; why do you infect yourself with them?

ROSALIND Peace, you dull fool! I found them on a tree.

TOUCHSTONE Truly, the tree yields bad fruit.

He disappears. Celia holds out her paper to Rosalind.

CELIA   Trow you who hath done this?

ROSALIND   Is it a man?

CELIA   It is young Orlando that tripped up the wrestler's heels and your heart, both in an instant.

ROSALIND   Alas the day, what shall I do with my doublet and hose? How looked he?

CELIA   Soft, comes he not here?

They retire into concealment. Orlando and Jaques appear.

JAQUES   Rosalind is your love's name?

ORLANDO   Yes, just.

JAQUES   I do not like her name.

ORLANDO   There was no thought of pleasing you when she was christened.

JAQUES   What stature is she of?

ORLANDO   Just as high as my heart.

JAQUES   You are full of pretty answers. Farewell, good Signior Love.

Jaques goes off in disgust. Rosalind leans forward. Orlando is whittling a boat.

ROSALIND I pray you, what is't o'clock?

ORLANDO You should ask me what time o' day. There is no clock in the forest.

He puts his boat into the brook. A sheet with verses is the sail. Rosalind throws a pebble at the boat.

ORLANDO (*angrily*) What would you?

ROSALIND (*jumps down from her branch and points to a tree carved with 'Rosalind'*) There is a man haunts the forest, that abuses our young plants, hangs odes upon hawthorns and elegies on brambles, all deifying the name of Rosalind. If I could meet that fancy-monger, I would give him some good counsel.

ORLANDO I am he that is so love-shaked.

ROSALIND Love is merely a madness; yet I profess curing it by counsel.

ORLANDO Did you ever cure any so?

ROSALIND   Yes, one, and in this manner. He was to imagine me his love, his mistress; and I set him every day to woo me. At which time would I grieve, be proud, fantastical, apish, inconstant, full of tears, full of smiles, that I drave my suitor from his mad humour of love to a living humour of madness. And thus I cured him.

ORLANDO   I would not be cured, youth.

ROSALIND   I would cure you, if you would but call me Rosalind, and come every day to my cote and woo me.

Love grows in the forest fast as weeds. Even Touchstone has found himself a mate, and being of the spirit, he has mocked even himself with his choice. He has found a true country lass, as thick as mud.

| TOUCHSTONE | I will fetch up your goats, Audrey, as another poet did. Truly, I wish the gods had made thee poetical. |

TOUCHSTONE I will fetch up your goats, Audrey, as another poet did. Truly, I wish the gods had made thee poetical.

AUDREY I do not know what 'poetical' is. Is it honest?

TOUCHSTONE No truly; for the truest poetry is the most feigning.

AUDREY Well, I am not fair, and therefore I pray the gods make me honest.

TOUCHSTONE Truly, and to cast away honesty upon a foul slut were to put good meat into an unclean dish. But be it as it may be, I will marry thee.

Nearby their cottage, Rosalind and Celia await Orlando. He is late.

ROSALIND Never talk to me, I will weep.

CELIA Do, but consider that tears do not become a man.

ROSALIND Why did he swear he would come this morning, and comes not?

CELIA Nay certainly there is no truth in him.

ROSALIND Not true in love? You have heard him swear he was.

CELIA 'Was' is not 'is'.

Old Corin approaches.

CORIN	Mistress and master, you have oft enquired after the shepherd that complained of love –
CELIA	Well, and what of him?

Corin, with his finger to his lips, beckons. They creep forward, part some foliage and observe Silvius and his Phebe.

SILVIUS	Sweet Phebe, do not scorn me, do not Phebe! If ever you meet in some fresh cheek the power of fancy, then shall you know the wounds invisible that love's keen arrows make.
PHEBE	But till that time, come not thou near me; and when that time comes, afflict me with thy mocks, pity me not, as till that time, I shall not pity thee.
SILVIUS	Oh!
ROSALIND	(*coming forward*) And why, I pray you? Who might be your mother, that you insult, exult, and all at once, over the wretched? You foolish shepherd, wherefore do you follow her? Mistress, know yourself. Down on your knees, and thank heaven fasting for a good man's love; for I must tell you friendly in your ear, sell when you can, you are not for all markets.

PHEBE   Sweet youth, I pray you chide a year together, I had rather hear you chide than this man woo.

ROSALIND   I pray you do not fall in love with me, for I am falser than vows made in wine. (*She leaves.*)

PHEBE   (*gazing after Rosalind*) Who ever loved that loved not at first sight?

In another part of the forest. Rosalind is standing on a bridge across the brook. At last, Orlando arrives.

ORLANDO   My fair Rosalind, I come within an hour of my promise.

ROSALIND   Break an hour's promise in love!

ORLANDO   Pardon me, dear Rosalind.

ROSALIND   Nay, and you be so tardy, come no more in my sight. I had as lief been wooed of a snail. Am not I your Rosalind?

ORLANDO   I would take some joy to say you are, because I would be talking of her.

ROSALIND   Well, in her person, I say I will not have you.

ORLANDO   Then in mine own person, I die.

ROSALIND No, faith, men have died from time to time, and worms have eaten them, but not for love. But come now, I will be your Rosalind in a more coming-on disposition; and ask me what you will, I will grant it.

ORLANDO Then love me, Rosalind.

ROSALIND Ay, and twenty such. Now tell me how long you would have her after you have possessed her.

ORLANDO For ever and a day.

ROSALIND Say 'a day' without the 'ever'. No, no, Orlando, men are April when they woo, December when they wed; maids are May when they are maids, but the sky changes when they are wives.

ORLANDO But will my Rosalind do so?

ROSALIND By my life, she will do as I do.

The sound of a horn is heard.

ORLANDO I must attend the duke at dinner. For these two hours I will leave thee. Adieu.

He departs. Celia appears from behind a tree.

CELIA You have simply misused our sex in your love-prate.

ROSALIND (*taking off her hat, fluffing out her hair, and lying on the grass*) O coz, coz, coz, my pretty little coz, that thou didst know how many fathom deep I am in love!

There is yet another victim of Duke Frederick's fury in the forest. Oliver de Boys, sent to fetch his brother, has wandered, lost and wretched, till at last he lies down to rest. As he sleeps, a lioness approaches. Then it is that Orlando, coming upon his brother, and seeing his danger, fights with the lioness and overcomes it. But in so doing, Orlando is wounded himself. Faint from loss of blood, he sends Oliver to keep his appointment with the shepherd boy. All enmity between the brothers is now ended.

OLIVER Good morrow, fair ones. Orlando doth commend him to you both. He sent me hither, stranger as I am, to tell this story, that you might excuse his broken promise, and to give this napkin, dy'd in his blood, unto the shepherd youth that he in sport doth call his Rosalind.

He holds out the napkin. Rosalind faints.

CELIA Why, how now, Ganymede, sweet Ganymede?

Celia and Oliver rush to help Rosalind up, but bump their heads together and, blushing, stare at each other.

OLIVER   Many will swoon when they do look on blood.

ROSALIND   I would I were at home.

They help her back to the cottage.

There is a haystack in a clearing. Voices come from it.

TOUCHSTONE   We shall find a time, Audrey, patience, gentle Audrey.

CORIN   (*entering and knocking on the haystack*) Our master and mistress seeks you. Come away, away!

TOUCHSTONE   (*to Audrey, who has run out and is putting herself in order*) Trip, Audrey, trip Audrey! I attend, I attend.

A clearing in the forest. Oliver and Orlando are together. Orlando's arm is in a sling.

ORLANDO   Is't possible that on so little acquaintance you should like her?

OLIVER   I love Aliena; she loves me; consent with both that we may enjoy each other. My father's house and all the revenue that was old Sir Rowland's will I estate upon you, and here live and die a shepherd.

ORLANDO   Let your wedding be tomorrow; thither will I invite the duke and all's contented followers.

Off goes Oliver, delighted. Rosalind appears.

ROSALIND   O my dear Orlando, how it grieves me to see thee wear thy heart in a scarf.

ORLANDO   It is my arm.

ROSALIND   Did your brother tell you how well I counterfeited to swoon when he showed me your handkercher?

ORLANDO   Ay, and greater wonders than that.

ROSALIND   O, I know where you are. Nay, 'tis true. Your brother and my sister are in the very wrath of love.

ORLANDO   They shall be married tomorrow. But O, how bitter a thing it is to look into happiness through another man's eyes!

ROSALIND   Why then tomorrow I cannot serve your turn for Rosalind?

ORLANDO   I can no longer live by thinking.

ROSALIND   (*mysteriously*) I can do strange things. Put you in your best array, bid your friends; for if you will be married tomorrow, you shall; and to Rosalind, if you will.

Silvius and Phebe appear.

PHEBE   Youth, you have done me much ungentleness –

ROSALIND   I care not if I have. You are there followed by a faithful shepherd – look upon him, love him; he worships you.

PHEBE   Good shepherd, tell this youth what 'tis to love.

SILVIUS   It is to be all made of sighs and tears, and so am I for Phebe.

PHEBE   And I for Ganymede.

ORLANDO   And I for Rosalind.

ROSALIND   And I for no woman.

SILVIUS   It is to be all made of faith and service, and so am I for Phebe.

PHEBE   And I for Ganymede.

ORLANDO   And I for Rosalind.

ROSALIND   And I for no woman.

SILVIUS   It is to be all made of fantasy, all made of passion –

ROSALIND   Pray you no more of this, 'tis like the howling of Irish wolves against the moon! (*To Phebe*) I will marry you if ever I marry woman, and I'll be married tomorrow. But if you do refuse to marry me, you'll give yourself to this most faithful shepherd.

PHEBE   So is the bargain.

ROSALIND   Keep your word; from hence I go to make these doubts all even. Tomorrow meet me all together.

The morning sun breaks through into a clearing. A flute plays.
Duke Senior, Jaques, Orlando, Oliver and Celia are waiting.

AMIENS   (*singing*)   It was a lover and his lass,
With a hey and a ho and a hey nonino,
That o'er the green corn-field did pass,
In spring-time, the only pretty ring-time,
When birds do sing, hey ding a ding, ding,
Sweet lovers love the spring.

DUKE SENIOR   Dost thou believe, Orlando, that Ganymede can do all this that he hath promised?

ORLANDO   I sometimes do believe, and sometimes do not.

Touchstone and Audrey, Silvius and Phebe enter.

JAQUES   There is sure another flood toward, and these couples are coming to the ark.

TOUCHSTONE   I press in here, sir, to swear and forswear, according as marriage binds and blood breaks. (*Pushing Audrey forward*) A poor virgin, sir, an ill-favoured thing, sir, but mine own.

Hymen enters.

HYMEN   Good Duke, receive thy daughter,
Hymen from heaven brought her,
That thou mightst join her hand with his
Whose heart within his bosom is.

He beckons and Rosalind, now dressed as herself, appears.

ROSALIND   (*to duke*) To you I give myself, for I am yours.
(*To Orlando*) To you I give myself for I am yours.

DUKE SENIOR   If there be truth in sight, you are my daughter.

ORLANDO   If there be truth in sight, you are my Rosalind.

PHEBE   If sight and shape be true, why then my love adieu!

HYMEN   Here's eight that must take hands,
To join in Hymen's bands.
(To Orlando and Rosalind)
You and you no cross shall part.
(To Oliver and Celia)
You and you are heart in heart.
(To Phebe)
You to his love must accord,
Or have a woman for your lord.
(To Touchstone and Audrey)
You and you are sure together,
As the winter to foul weather.

The couples embrace. A messenger enters.

MESSENGER   Let me have audience for a word or two. Duke Frederick
addressed a mighty power to take his brother here, and to the
skirts of this wild wood he came. Meeting with an old religious
man, he was converted from his enterprise and from the world,
his crown bequeathing to his banished brother.

DUKE SENIOR   Every of this happy number that have endur'd shrewd days and nights with us, shall share the good of our returned fortune . . . Play, music, and you brides and bridegrooms all, with measure heap'd in joy, to th' measures fall!

As the curtain falls, the couples pass before the spectators in joyful dancing.